SOMERSET

The Glorious County

T O N Y   H O W E L L

First published in Great Britain in 2008

Copyright © Tony Howell 2008

British Library Cataloguing-in-Publication Data
A CIP record for this title is available from the British Library

ISBN 978 1 84114 759 8

HALSGROVE
Halsgrove House
Ryelands Industrial Estate
Bagley Road, Wellington, Somerset TA21 9PZ
Tel: 01823 653777   Fax: 01823 216796
email: sales@halsgrove.com
website: www.halsgrove.com

Printed and bound by
Grafiche Flaminia, Italy

INTRODUCTION

Somerset has such a wonderfully diverse range of landscapes, from rugged coastline to rolling green hills, and from long sandy beaches to endless acres of wetlands, making it an ideal subject for artists.

From Wells, the smallest city in England, to Bath, one of the most attractive cities in the world, the architecture and history here rivals any other county in Britain.

Other famous towns include Glastonbury, famous for much more than just the world's biggest music festival, with the majestic ruins of the Abbey, the Chalice Well gardens and the iconic landmark of Glastonbury Tor as just some of its gems. Taunton is the county town, and the largest town in Somerset, famous for its County Cricket and marvellous churches.

Facing west, the coast receives the good and bad weather blown over from the Atlantic, and looks out to spectacular sunsets all year round. The golden sandy beaches in the north give way to rockier shores in the south, until you get to Minehead, ideally located with the blue sea on one side, and the picturesque Exmoor National Park on the other.

Agriculture is one of the main businesses in the county, with farming remaining popular, giving us milk, wool and famous cheeses (not just Cheddar) to compete with the other product popularly associated with Somerset – cider, which is produced from the multitude of apple orchards found here.

The famous English poet Coleridge lived here in Nether Stowey, and was inspired to write some of his finest work, and the composer Holst (born up the road in Cheltenham) wrote his 'Somerset Rhapsody' after visiting the county. This inspiring quality carries on today, influencing many artists, myself included, as I have tried to capture the beauty of Somerset, the glorious county.

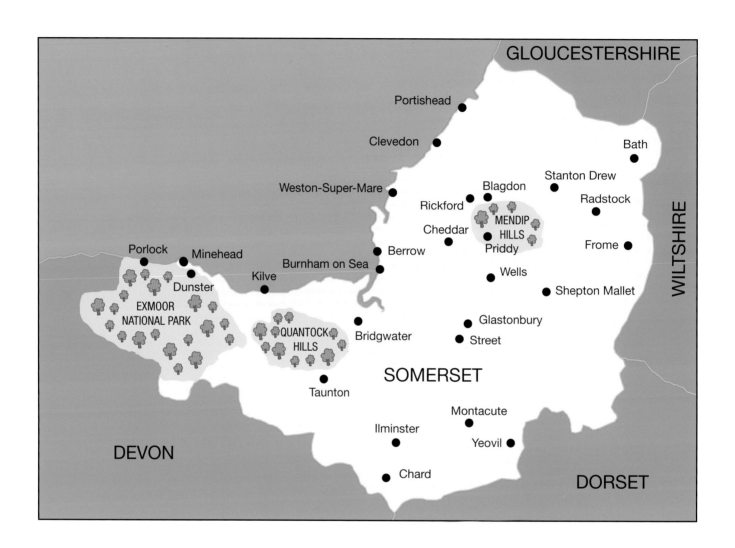

GLOUCESTERSHIRE

WILTSHIRE

DEVON

DORSET

Portishead

Clevedon

Bath

Weston-Super-Mare

Stanton Drew

Blagdon

Radstock

Rickford

MENDIP HILLS

Cheddar

Frome

Priddy

Porlock   Minehead

Berrow

Burnham on Sea

Wells

Dunster

Kilve

Shepton Mallet

EXMOOR NATIONAL PARK

Glastonbury

Bridgwater

Street

QUANTOCK HILLS

SOMERSET

Taunton

Montacute

Ilminster

Yeovil

Chard

People line the streets in November to watch the illuminated Bridgwater Carnival.

This delightful cottage is in Montacute village, near Yeovil.

St Andrew Northover church at Ilchester is situated above the road, almost as if on a pedestal.

Rock of Ages, Burrington Combe. The inscription reads 'This rock derives its name from the well known hymn written about 1762 by the Rev. A M Toplady who was inspired whilst sheltering in this cleft during a storm'.

Cricket House, Cricket St Thomas where the BBC TV series *To the Manor Born* was filmed.

A small pine tree battles to survive against the regular strong winds on the Quantock Hills.

Dawn comes late to the River Brue estuary on a cold but peaceful January morning.

Winter trees on the Brendon Hills, on the edge of Exmoor National Park.

A flock of rooks scavenges for food on the fields below Dunster Castle near Minehead.

The historic thatched Toll House on the A30, just outside the town of Chard.

The original Manor House in the small village of Meare, soon to be refurbished by English Heritage.

The Market Cross at Shepton Mallet dates back to the 1500s.

The large Victorian stately home on the Orchardleigh estate near Frome, which also has a lake with an island church.

Thatched cottages line Church Steps at Minehead, on the way up to
St Michael's church, which has great views over the town.

Sunset reflected in the calm waters of the River Parrett estuary near Steart Island.

Coppiced willow trees (salix) are commonly grown on the Somerset Levels,
and used for basket making, fences and garden sculptures.

Lone sheep and beech tree on a hill near Curry Rivel.

King Solomon's Temple is a spectacular sight within Gough's Cave at Cheddar.

The majestic region of Cheddar Gorge known as 'The Pinnacles'
reflecting light from a full moon, under a carpet of stars in January.

A car travels down Cheddar Gorge towards the town, under a moody sky.
Rockfalls have often closed this road in the past, but are less common these days.

In spring the grass and trees at Cheddar Gorge take on a bright fresh appearance. The peaks shown here are known as The Pinnacles, a favourite place for the more daring rock climbers. They are much taller in real life than photographs make them appear.

Goats were introduced to Cheddar Gorge for scrub control in the 1990s. Cheddar supports a fine range of flora which was threatened when sheep grazing ceased in the 1970s. This one is chewing, not calling.

Mistletoe on a tree
near Curry Rivel in February.

Cider is probably the one thing most popularly associated with Somerset.
The apple trees start to blossom in late in April.

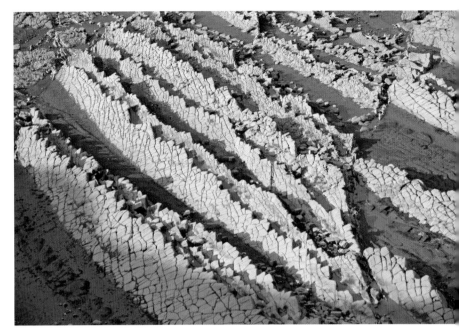

The shelves and steps leading back from the shoreline on Kilve Beach, taken from the cliffs above.

Twisted cliff formations and shelves on Kilve Beach.

The wooden lighthouse on the beach at Burnham on Sea. Built in 1832 and still in use today.

This image shows the lighthouse at Burnham on Sea, above which the island of
Flat Holm is just visible. The larger island on the left is Steep Holm, a bird sanctuary.

Wreck of *The Nornen*, a Norwegian barque
which was driven on to Berrow Beach in 1897.

Berrow Sands lie between Brean and Burnham on Sea, and are
a haven for wild shore birds, as the tide goes so far out each day
exposing huge mudflats for them to feed on.

Inside St Mary's church, Burnham on Sea which has a famous leaning tower.

In the parish of St Andrew's near Burnham on Sea lies the charming Edithmead church, made of corrugated iron. Shown here at Christmas time.

The Harvest Moon is the first full moon after the autumnal equinox. Here the strong moonlight has sidelighted the ripples in the sand left by the receding tide at Burnham on Sea.

People walking their dog along Brean Beach, taken from the top of Brean Down, a mile-long promontory in the Bristol Channel.

Brean Down peninsula, managed by the National Trust, from Marine Lake, Weston-Super-Mare.

Vicars Close, Wells is said to be the oldest planned street in Europe.
At one end there is a stairway which took the vicars to the cathedral via a covered bridge.

Bishop's Palace gatehouse and moat at
Wells take on a more spooky appearance at night.

The magnificent west front of Wells Cathedral at night. Completed
in 1250, it is 100 feet high and 150 feet wide. Almost 300 of the
medieval figure sculptures remain, and most are larger than lifesize.

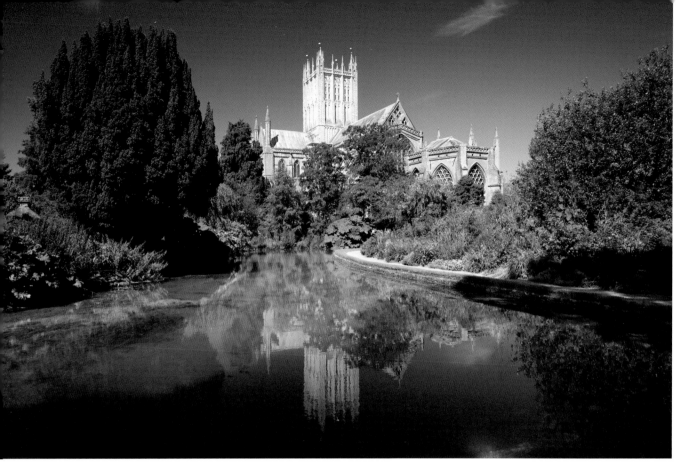

Above: Wells Cathedral from the Bishop's Palace. This is where the spring wells up, giving the town its name.

Left: Chapter House, Wells Cathedral was the place where all the business relating to the cathedral was decided.

44

Early morning sun melts the frost away at this church at Rickford, near the Mendip Hills.

Above: Buzzards are a common sight over Somerset nowadays. This one was being chased off by a crow.

Left: Blagdon Lake on a clear bright day in early spring.

47

Cows search for grass among the frosty ground on a
cold winter's morning near Blagdon.

Willow drying by the side of a stream
near Curry Rivel, on the Somerset Levels.

View over a calm Blagdon Lake from the Mendip Hills, with St Andrew's church in the foreground.

Above: Priddy Ponds is an area in the Mendip Hills, once mined by the Romans for lead. These tall grasses were pictured in October, when they turn orangey-brown.

Overleaf: This was taken after a rare snowfall in March, at the very pretty Priddy Ponds in the Mendip Hills.

Beech trees in a line at Draycott Sleights Nature Reserve on the Mendip Hills.

A Scots pine tree leans over in peaty soil on the Somerset Levels. In the distance is Crooks Peak, part of the Mendip Hills.

Young bull and rain-filled clouds at Lower Weare, near the River Axe, at the foot of the Mendips.

Crooks Peak (628ft) is a prominent part of the Mendip range of hills.

St Nicholas's church has a glorious setting at Uphill, the seaward end
of the Mendip Hills. On the horizon is the Welsh mainland.

The Grand Pier at Weston-Super-Mare on a foggy November night.

After the first frost of winter, cows search for food in a field on the Mendip Hills at sunrise.

Opposite: A long shutter speed of 32 seconds makes the clouds blur as they move over Glastonbury Tor at night.

Above: Glastonbury Abbey is reputed to be the oldest above-ground Christian church in the world. Legend has it that King Arthur is buried here.

Left: The town of Street starts to awaken to a frosty morning, with Glastonbury Tor making the perfect backdrop.

Overleaf: Canada Geese cruise the waters of Wimbleball Lake, Exmoor, on a calm winter's day.

Late August near Dunkery Beacon, the highest point on Exmoor, sees the heather at its peak flowering time near a solitary hawthorn tree.

Exmoor ponies graze on the shore of Wimbleball Lake.

Tarr Steps is a prehistoric bridge over the River Barle near Hawkridge, Exmoor. Dating from 1000 BC, some of the stones weigh 5 tons yet still wash away in storms, hence they've been numbered to facilitate rebuilding.

Somerset has many small roads like this one on Exmoor; lined with trees,
making driving so much more pleasurable in every season.

Midsummer, and all of Somerset turns a luscious green, including this ash tree overlooking Lansdown near Bath.

The magnificent Bath Abbey and the Roman Baths illuminated at dusk.

The new Thermae Spa at Bath attracts international visitors to bathe in its warm waters.

Above: The world famous Pulteney Bridge, Bath, bathed in early morning
sunshine as the River Avon cascades over Pulteney Weir.

Opposite: The spectacular north side of Bath Abbey at dusk in summer.

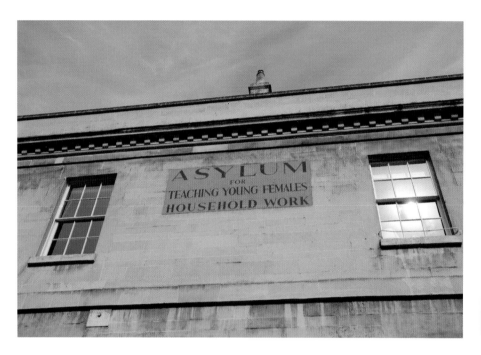

Above: 'Asylum for teaching young females household work' old sign on a Georgian building in Bath.

Opposite: Last light on the majestic Royal Crescent, in the second most-visited place (after Windsor) outside London – Bath of course.

Top: Fresh new iris leaves on a lake at Shapwick Heath in April.

Above: A host of dancing daffodils on a verge at Minehead, West Somerset.

Opposite: The Abbot's Fish House at Meare, which once had large fishing ponds nearby.

Golden willow trees adorned with new leaves at the village of Isle Brewers.

The Burton Pynsent Monument was erected by the former Prime Minister William Pitt the Elder to the memory of Sir William Pynsent, who had left the Burton Pynsent Estate to Pitt in thanks for his opposition to the imposition of a tax on cider.

A group of fir trees on the Quantock Hills, a place favoured by many locals for a good walk – whatever the weather.

Ashton Windmill was a flour mill, and stands on the Isle of Wedmore, a large ridge giving views over the Somerset Levels. Captured here on a frosty November morning at sunrise.

The sun sets behind Ashton Windmill, on the Isle of Wedmore overlooking the Somerset Levels.

Houses by the River Tone at Burrowbridge
on a cold January night.

The illuminated church on Burrow Mump reflecting in
the River Parrett on a clear, cold night in January.

Burrow Mump, which holds the ruin of St Michael's church, rises up above the Somerset Levels much like Glastonbury Tor.

A rainbow over the lake on the sea front at Portishead.

Overleaf: This line of bare beech trees look black against a layer of snow on the Quantock Hills.

Top: A relic from the Second World War, this 'Pill Box' has gradually sunk into the pebbles at Porlock Weir, on the edge of Exmoor.

Above: Picturesque boats and cottages at high tide, Porlock Weir.

Opposite: Boat at sunset near Pawlett, on the banks of the River Parrett estuary.

Reeds at dawn on a lake at Shapwick Heath, the Somerset Levels.

The Dovecote dates from the sixteenth century, and overlooks Bruton, said to be the smallest town in England.

The splendid Marina at the revitalised Portishead, near Bristol.

A very foggy day in December makes the end of Clevedon Pier invisible.

Taunton Castle was originally a Saxon site, and is now the home of the County Museum. The old castle fell into ruin, but was restored to great effect. By day, the castle is a wonderful sight in its town centre location.

At night, Taunton Castle takes on a much more mysterious appearance, more in keeping with myths and legends.

The Museum of Somerset is housed inside Taunton Castle. On the right is a replica of the castle keep.

A calm evening in Taunton, which allows the River Tone to reflect perfectly the ornate Tone Bridge and surroundings.

Stained glass windows at the beautiful
St Mary Magdalene church, Taunton.

St Mary Magdalene church in Hammet Street, Taunton
has one of the finest towers in Somerset, with statues all around.

Top: Dairy cows make the most of the plentiful grazing at Brent Knoll in May.

Above: Lambs are a common sight all over Somerset, from December through to the end of summer. This trio were photographed in February at Edithmead, near Burnham on Sea.

Opposite: Standing Stones at the Great Circle, Stanton Drew. A recent geophysical survey showed the megalithic remains are just the ruin of a much more elaborate site, yet to be excavated.

97

A fifteenth century thatched cottage, once used as the Toll House, at Stanton Drew village.

A pond near Westhay on the Somerset Levels in February.

A lake at Shapwick Heath in February, with Glastonbury Tor on the horizon.

Above: A wheat field in July, near Corston, North Somerset.

Right: The house sparrow is still a regular sight in Somerset, despite their seemingly ever-decreasing numbers.

The glorious fern-leaved beech tree at Bath Botanical Gardens.

An oak tree in an oilseed rape field near Chelwood, North East Somerset. Rape has been a popular rotation crop since the 1970s, grown to make vegetable oil and more.

Flax field near Corston, North East Somerset. Flax seeds are highly nutritious and contain oil which is beneficial to arthritis sufferers.

Hawkweed and poppies growing together on the edge of a field near Farmborough, North Somerset.

In the small village of Muchelney stands the Abbot's House, the only large structure
remaining of Muchelney Abbey, a former Benedictine monastery.

Stembridge Tower Mill, at High Ham, is the last remaining thatched windmill in England.

The church of St Peter and St Paul at North Curry village. It is nicknamed 'the Cathedral of the Moors' because of its commanding setting overlooking Curry Moor, part of the Somerset Levels.

The sea front graveyard of St Andrew's church, Clevedon illuminated by a full moon in August, with the lights of South Wales giving a yellow glow on the horizon.

Young bulls are always inquisitive when I enter their fields,
and are difficult to photograph because they come right up to me.
There was a river between us when I took this shot; this gave me
a chance to capture them at a short distance.

The stone circle on Ham Hill (near Yeovil) was built especially for
the millennium; to commemorate many centuries of quarrying
on the hill, and the men who worked there.

Barford House is now a private dwelling. It lies in the village of Enmore, 2 miles to the west of Bridgwater.

St Mary's church and the Cornhill, Bridgwater at dusk with traffic trails from commuters on their way home.

The wonderfully named Temple of Harmony is in the grounds of
Halswell House, on the edge of the Quantock Hills.

A lone tree growing on a round hill near Farmborough, North East Somerset.

Rolling fields and round hill near Farmborough, North East Somerset.

Winter silver birch trees on the edge of Hawkridge Reservoir, north of the Quantock Hills.

The Hood Monument near Butleigh. Built in the nineteenth century, the monument commemorates the career of a local boy who left home at fourteen to join the Navy, and later became an admiral. It was linked to the family home by an avenue of cedar trees, some of which still stand today.

Downside Abbey is a place of worship for the nearby school and the public, but is also where monks spend two hours every day in prayer. It's in the village of Stratton-on-the-Fosse, near Radstock, North East Somerset.

This old mining wheel stands outside the museum at Radstock, one of the
best-preserved mining heritage towns left in England.

Wisteria floribunda hangs its beautiful foliage down the side of Forde Abbey, located on the South Somerset border near Devon.

The secluded location of Forde Abbey, on the South Somerset border, previously a monastery (dating back to 1148), now a private home open to the public.

Above: A classic view of Birnbeck Pier at Weston-Super-Mare,
where the local lifeboats are launched from. It is in need of repair and is due for renovation.

Opposite: A fine example of a bluebell wood surrounded by beech trees, at Cleeve Hill Wood, near Congresbury.

Top: Ivy's Cottage is set in one of Somerset's most picturesque villages, Selworthy near Minehead.

Above: Montacute House near Yeovil, with its honey-coloured stone, is one of the finest Elizabethan Country Houses in the UK. It is owned by the National Trust.

Opposite: An unusual cloud formation echoes the shapes of the hill at Draycott Sleights Nature Reserve near Cheddar.

Above: Stunning autumn trees line one side of a field full of beetroot near Cannington.

Opposite: A lone boat floats on a very calm sea reflecting the sunset, near the Quantock Hills.

Above: Gorgeous pink sunset clouds surround the moon in its 'waxing crescent' phase over Bath, North East Somerset.

Opposite: The setting summer sun illuminates the side of Clevedon Pier with a golden glow.

Above: A typical Somerset farmhouse, nestled in between patchwork fields near Nether Stowey, on the northern edge of the Quantock Hills.

Opposite: Known locally as 'The Magnificent Seven', these beech trees form a distinctive landmark near Horner on Exmoor.

St Audrie's church looks so picturesque, nestling into the hillside as it does near St Audrie's Bay, West Somerset.

Summer's day view of patchwork fields from Winsford Hill, in the heart of Exmoor.

Above: A tree perfectly silhouetted against a glorious summer sunset near Marksbury, North East Somerset.

Opposite: The island of Steep Holm, seen here from Marine Lake, Weston-Super-Mare,
is a bird and nature sanctuary. It can be visited during summer months by boat from Weston.

Dawn brings bright colours behind the silhouette of St Mary's church at East Brent, a small village in the Sedgemoor area.

Opposite: An ash tree in the snow near Bath, with the appropriately named Freezing Hill on the horizon. The line of beech trees on Freezing Hill is a landmark visible for miles around.

I know what you're thinking: 'I thought this was a Somerset book, not Cornwall?' Burrow Farm Iron Mine engine house, near Brompton Regis, Exmoor, was based on the Cornish tin mine design, but is nowehere near Cornwall.

Opposite: View in late evening sunlight on the Somerset/Wiltshire border outside Bath, North East Somerset.

A young oak tree growing on the side of the Polden Hills
near Street, on a misty morning in November.

Right: Bare winter trees and frost on the Polden Hills
as fog covers the valley below.

Lilstock was used as a port in the eighteenth century for exporting lime, and these wooden posts are all that remain of the pier that once stood here.

Willow Man is a sculpture made by artist Serena de la Hey on the edge of the M5 Motorway near Bridgwater.
It measures 12 metres high and is possibly the largest willow sculpture in the world.
Willow is a crop very much associated with the glorious Somerset Levels.